C000138616

DEF LEPPARD

ORION

AN ORION PAPERBACK

This is a Carlton Book

First published in Great Britain in 1994 by Orion Books Ltd, Orion House,
5 Upper St Martin's Lane, London, WC2H 9EA.

Text and design © 1994 Carlton Books Ltd
CD Guide format © 1994 Carlton Books Ltd

A CIP catalogue record for this book is available from the British Library.

ISBN 1 85797 929 X

Edited, designed and typeset by Archetype Ltd.
Printed in Italy

THE AUTHOR

Jason Rich, 25, lives in Kent, England. He has been a trainee railway technician, a writer, an acoustic
guitarist and a singer. He lived in Portugal before joining the Royal Navy where he narrowly escaped being
torpedoed. He then studied political and social history. His hobbies include drinking with the lads.

CONTENTS

INTRODUCTION

The time is 8.45 pm on Sunday, August 24, 1980. The place is the Reading Rock festival—in truth a muddy field, in a not-very-inspiring part of the English countryside. Within a few years it will become a mecca for the alternative and independent music scene, but this year it is still a predominantly rock-based

Phil Collen adds guitar dynamite to Leppard.

> **"We're all posers. We go on stage, pose, wear dinky white boots, tight trousers and have all the girls looking at our bollocks."**
> *Rick Savage*

6

extravaganza containing 40,000 damp and jaded fans. Among the acts playing this weekend are a group of young British musicians who have just returned from a first—and stunningly successful—American tour. They are about to play their set: a carefully rehearsed collection of songs that represent all the hard work they've done since early days spent rehearsing in the grim and draughty environs of an old, abandoned spoon factory.

Darkness is falling and the festival site becomes a weird, almost medieval scene, as bonfires burn amid a sea of fluttering flags and banners, waved aloft by the

A long way from the spoon factory

encamped army of drunken ruffians. A million miles from the sun-drenched shores of exciting America, the incredibly young band, clad only in shorts and tee shirts, shiver in the cold night air. But they play. The sound is excellent, the lighting superb and they play well. It is obvious that they are streets ahead of all the other so-called metal bands on the bill. They have dynamic arrangements, make clever use of acoustic guitar sections and they play together with tight

Def Leppard—no strangers to tabloid headlines

professionalism.

A considerable section of the audience are impressed, but as the set progresses it seems that the singer's vocal exhortations are falling on deaf ears—particularly those near the front: there is virtually no reaction to a succession of songs, beyond a solitary cry of "piss off".

The guitarist pleads desperately with the crowd: "Let's hear some noise then."

"Fuck off!" is all he gets in return for his pains.

The band line up in their classic heads-down-and-boogie pose and reach a musical climax… which is greeted with a large round of indifference. They leave without any applause and, too shell-shocked to cut their losses, come back for an unwarranted encore that earns them a chorus of boos.

Two-and-a-half years after this

> **"Deaf Leopard was the name of an imaginary band that came to life."**
> *Joe Elliott*

shattering experience Def Leppard's album *Pyromania* was to begin a 92-week run in the US Hot 100, reaching Number 2—it was only held off the Number 1 spot by Michael Jackson's *Thriller*. It eventually sold seven million copies in the US.

It even reached Number 18 in the UK Top 20 but, as the boys knew only too well by then, the faint praise they received at home could never match the fame they enjoyed abroad—particularly in the US. This is the story of how Def Leppard made America sit up and listen…

9

SHEFFIELD STEEL

Rock'n'roll dreams, and a hell-bent determination to turn them into reality: these were the driving forces behind the evolution of Def Leppard. They weren't alone, there were scores of young rock bands in various stages of development in Britain in the late-Seventies.

Flying in the face of punk, the New Wave Of British Heavy Metal (as it rather cumbersomely came to be known) was made up of young, hard-rock bands who rose up as icons for part of that generation who weren't into green hair and anarchy in the UK. Many of the bands, like Sledgehammer and Weapon, are no more than metal memories now, although bands like Iron Maiden and Girlschool thundered on for many more years. Today, another resurgence of even more extreme music has come with the genuinely disturbing advent of 'death metal' bands, of which some European outfits are worryingly into living the satanistic sort imagery they employ.

But of the NWOBHM bands in the late-Seventies, out to rock and

> ## "I couldn't play an instrument and I couldn't sing. But I looked good!"
> *Joe Elliott*

Let's Get Rocked!

Joe Elliott and Steve Clark

have a good time, few had the single-minded drive and vision of the tight-knit bunch of school friends and college mates who came together in the north of England to turn their fantasies into reality—no easy task when you're struggling to make it in the long shadow of the steel mills of Sheffield, Yorkshire.

Sheffield was world famous for its steel and cutlery industries. Amid the heat and smoke, it produced tough people and, inevitably, its musical output was noted for its cutting edge. The raucous soul singer Joe Cocker is one of Sheffield's best known musical exports, as are important pop acts like the Human League, Comsat Angels, and Heaven 17.

But Def Leppard with their polished brand of heavy metal, sharp as a Sheffield knife, would become

> **"My mum and dad were the first people to believe in us."**
> *Joe Elliott*

one of the city's most successful bands against all the odds, and, in the process, help keep alive the spirit of British rock during a decade of fierce competition. Their musical idealism also provided them with an escape route from the easy monotony and grind of dead-end jobs, or worse, unemployment in a period of industrial decline.

They would ultimately experience both triumphs and disasters, but came together for the best possible reasons. In the finest traditions of the local "beat group" that stretch back to the birth of the Beatles, they simply wanted to make music they believed in and to have fun. They also wanted to make it on their own terms.

Metal rebels

That meant producing their own demos and playing frantic, anxious gigs to handfuls of friends and supporters in school halls and clubs. It was a gestation period, a trying-

Fellow famous Sheffield band the Human League

13

*Led Zeppelin—
role models for
Def Leppard*

out time during which various hopeful musicians came and went.

At the time the founder members got together, the British scene was dominated by a mixture of post-Bowie glam bands and Seventies supergroups. Then, just as Def Leppard began to emerge from their musty rehearsal room to face the world, there was a violent sea change. Overnight, punk rock undermined the whole edifice carefully built up over the previous decade. In the wake of the Sex Pistols' *Never Mind The Bollocks*, safety pins and spitting fans, even— almost unthinkably—the mighty Led Zeppelin seemed redundant. But there was still a vast audience for hard rock and heavy metal, and there was a breed of young players who felt punk was an irrelevant fashion trend.

The proto-Leppards might have liked the rebellious excitement of 'Pretty Vacant' and perhaps approved of the democratization of the record-making process. But they didn't want to snarl their way through three angry chords. Brought up on Mott The Hoople, Rush, Sweet, Thin Lizzy, and UFO, they wanted songs and solos as well as energy and attitude.

Critical days

The first squallings of the new band came in the shape of an outfit called Atomic Mass, whose lineup went through a bewildering number of changes before anything remotely recognizable as Leppard-like emerged. The prime mover was Rick Savage (born December 2, 1960). He had got his first guitar at

Sheffield—city of steel

> **"We try to look good and have style."**
> *Rick Allen*

the age of ten and learned chords and a few simple rock standards. His other major passion was soccer: he had played for Sheffield Schools and at the age of 14 signed with the junior team for one of the big local clubs—Sheffield United. But he didn't enjoy life among professional soccer players and became more interested in the music business.

A fan of Sweet and Slade, he put together his first group with a drummer friend, Tony Kenning. Armed with a new electric guitar, "Sav" brought in another guitarist called Peter Doubleday and singer Nicholas McKay, both of whom eventually faded from the scene. They had no bass player but cheerfully rehearsed in Kenning's parents' house, working out cover versions of Queen songs.

Pete Willis (born February 16, 1960) had attended Tapton Comprehensive—the same school as

> ## "We were not into punk. We were all heavy rock fans before we formed this band."
> *Rick Savage*

Rick—and was invited along to play guitar with the fledgling group at the local youth club. Pete also brought along a bass player called Paul Hampshire. Now they had the chance to play together, performing the music of favourite bands like T Rex and Thin Lizzy.

Atomic Mass was born.

Raw recruits

Willis had been hooked on rock guitar since, at the age of eight, he had seen Jimi Hendrix on TV. He made his own imitation guitar and posed with it in front of the

Joe the singer

bedroom mirror, until he got his first proper electric at the age of 12. He was undoubtedly a better guitarist than Rick and he listened to more mature rock music too, enjoying albums by Pink Floyd and Santana.

Encouraged by a school teacher who heard the boys playing, Atomic Mass put on their first show for friends and fellow pupils in the school gymnasium. Although they didn't know it, in the audience was an intrigued Joe Elliott—a future Leppard lynchpin. He watched as the band played covers of hits by Led Zeppelin, Queen, Slade, and the Who.

The boys were due to leave school in the summer of 1977, and after working in a supermarket for a while, Pete got a job with British Oxygen as a junior draughtsman, while "Sav" and Tony went to work for British Rail. But Rick Savage,

no neighbours and they could make as much noise as they liked. Bliss!

Hey Joe

The need for a singer became more pressing and the answer to the band's prayers was the youngster who'd watched their school performance—Joe Elliott (born August 1, 1959). Joe worked as a van driver and Pete had known him ever since chance meetings at the local youth club. After various discussions about "starting a band", Savage, Tony and Pete asked Joe if he'd like to join. When he promised to help pay for rehearsals and a PA system, he was enrolled before he'd even sung a note!

Every Friday night after work or college they jammed and rehearsed with drummer Kenning until the early hours. In November 1977 they formed the first line up of Def Leppard, based on the name Deaf

> "Heavy metal grew up and that had to happen. We put a lot more melodies and harmonies into our music."
> *Rick Savage*

Pete Willis and Tony Kenning agreed to stay together to keep Atomic Mass alive, with Rick switching to bass and Pete playing all the lead guitar. All they needed now was a lead singer…

Now that they had left school they could no longer rehearse at the Tapton youth club and were getting too big and too loud to play at home. In September 1977 Tony found a disused spoon factory, in Bramall Lane—they rented it for £5 a night (about $10). It was a cold, uncomfortable place, but there were

Future Joe: Would the early singer have recognized this successful Nineties' star?

19

> **"If you are going to last beyond a couple of years, you've got to be there all the time."**
> *Pete Willis*

At the first rehearsal Joe sang a version of Led Zeppelin's 'Stairway To Heaven'. After playing some other songs by David Bowie and Thin Lizzy, they decided it would be more productive to try to write their own material. Their first song, with lyrics by Elliott, was 'Misty Dreamer'—which turned into a seven-minute epic and became the springboard for all their future work. It later resurfaced on the band's first album, re-arranged as 'Sorrow Is A Woman'.

"My only problem when I joined Def Leppard," said Joe later, "was that I couldn't play an instrument and I couldn't sing. But I looked good! All I'd ever done was sing in the choir and in the bath. They picked me to join Atomic Mass because I looked right. I was tall and I had long hair and I didn't look wimpy. I didn't know how to sing rock'n'roll, but I was

Leopard, which had been dreamed up at school by their new singer. Joe had spent hours writing imaginary reviews of his dream band and had even produced posters—long before he had ever sung with a group!

Their new front man was tall, blond and good looking, and although he had a tendency to be overweight, his was just the face they needed for a dynamic front man. Unfortunately, Joe couldn't sing too well—as he freely admitted. But he could shout and yell and pose and he could learn to get his voice in shape—and in tune.

Ted Nugent encouraged Def Leppard when they first hit America.

enthusiastic. I was lucky they stuck with me while I learned how to sing. Performing live is what I love best. I love a show with lots of excitement."

Guitar harmony

By Christmas the band had enough material, including covers, to put on a show for their friends at the rehearsal room. It went well, and they were even asked to play their first ever encore. But at this early stage, the boys felt there was something missing from their sound. Pete was doing his best on lead guitar, but they needed something extra.

It was when Pete was flicking through a guitar manual in class at Stannington College, Sheffield that he was seen by another student called Steve Clark. Yes, he too played guitar. But it wasn't until they both met at a concert by Judas

"It were this big!"

Priest at Sheffield City Hall that they began serious discussions and realized that if they teamed up, they could emulate the twin harmony guitar sound that was the forte of their heroes Scott Gorham and Brian Robertson of Thin Lizzy.

Pete invited Steve along to a rehearsal at the spoon factory and after he played the solo from Lynyrd Skynyrd's 'Freebird' he was quickly brought in as their second guitarist. Steve was born in nearby Hillsborough on April 23, 1960. His parents were rock'n'roll fans and he grew up listening to their records. His father Barry gave him his first guitar at the age of 11 and he had classical lessons—which helped him later on when he inevitably wanted to copy 'Stairway To Heaven'.

His first rehearsal as a proper member of Def Leppard was on January 29, 1978. Although he didn't much like playing in the spoon factory he was most impressed by the band's determination to play their own material. The new twin-guitar line-up was much stronger with Pete playing heavy rhythmic riffs, Steve adding lead solos and helping to write new material which further boosted the band's progress. However Steve was working shifts as a lathe operator which disrupted the band's rehearsal schedules. He also became impatient at the lack of gigs. He threatened to leave the band unless they got work, and eventually Joe Elliott—ever the fixer and go-getter—contacted a friend who booked them to play at Westfield School, Sheffield. The gig was on July 18, 1978, and the band made their debut in front of 150 schoolkids. It didn't seem an auspicious start: Steve's amplifier wasn't switched on, so the first few

23

seconds of the opening number were lost, and later Joe forgot his lyrics. But the show was a success. They played for nearly an hour, all original material except for Thin Lizzy's 'Jailbreak' saved as a show-stopper for the encore.

They earned just £5 (about $10)—which paid for another rehearsal. But it was a good start. The band were thrilled at having finally achieved their first goal. They

"Pour some sugar on me!"

spent the next few months playing at low-paid school dances, youth club gigs and colleges, gaining invaluable experience.

On the record

The next major step came when the band played at a Sheffield club called the Limit. They were booked to play on September 11, 1979, on the first of two nights devoted to up-coming local talent and headlining on the same night as Def Leppard were a new electro-pop group called the Human League.

All the bands were given good reviews in the music press, except for Def Leppard who were criticized in *Record Mirror* for their "crass macho poses". Their music was dismissed as nothing but "bludgeon riffola". Even so it was admitted the band had been the most popular with the fans, and they were booked back to play at the Limit, billed as

> **"I was tall and I had long hair and I didn't look wimpy."**
> *Joe Elliott*

"The Young Kings Of Rock".

In the same month they were featured in the city's major evening newspaper *The Sheffield Star* and were highly praised as: "a five-piece revealing a rare maturity in their writing and playing as they punch out heavy rock originals with more than a nod to melody."

The next step was to make their own record. Borrowing from the punk tradition of do-it-yourself, Def Leppard decided to make their own. It was a big gamble to record, produce, finance and then distribute their own three-track EP (extended play) but they were determined to

25

keep the momentum going. The plan was to record at the Fairview Studios in Kingston-upon-Hull, Humberside. But, dramatically, a week before the session Def Leppard decided to fire their drummer Tony Kenning. It was a familiar rock'n'roll problem. Tony was a good player but he wanted to spend more time with his girlfriend.

"His heart wasn't in it," explained Rick Savage later. After missing a couple of rehearsals, Tony was out. It was a painful decision, but it had to be done. The band came first as far as Joe, Pete, Rick and Steve were concerned. Joe recruited another drummer, Frank Noon, for the session. Frank was with another Sheffield outfit called the Next Band, who had also recorded their own EP—Frank knew the ropes.

Despite the cost and the upheavals involved, making the EP

Would you believe this band would one day conquer the world?

which became known as *Getcha Rocks Off* was crucial to the ultimate success of Def Leppard—the band were determined to do it.

"We borrowed and stole enough money to finance a small eight-track studio to cut the EP," confessed Steve Clark later. Joe Elliott's parents also lent the band money to pay for the great experiment. It was a clever move because it earned Def Leppard a lot of respect for their enterprise, and it led directly to their getting a welcome blast of national publicity and a record contract with a major label. The three tracks 'Ride Into The Sun', 'Getcha Rocks Off' and 'The Overture' caused a sensation. Def Leppard was about to spring at the nation's throat.

Rick Savage slaps his bass.

GETCHA ROCKS OFF!

Punk and its anarchic heroes were far removed from the earthy world of working class rock, yet the young Sheffield rockers learned a lot from the rebellious, dispossessed musicians. They admired the way punk bands could actually get their music on record without the help of the hide-bound major record companies. It seemed like a good example—as heavy metal rock in the late-Seventies had gone underground and become unfashionable, getting out there and making it happen for themselves was the only way the band could crack it. With the innocence and energy of youth, Def Leppard set out to make their music hugely popular— whatever the dictates of fashion. *Getcha Rocks Off* was the key.

The sessions were held on November 25 and 26, 1978, and the music proved to be the basis of their future work, with the emphasis on melodic structures, clever guitar parts and driving rock beats behind vocal harmonies. There was plenty of space for Pete Willis and Steve Clark to shine on lead guitars and Joe sang his heart out, climaxing with a mighty scream at the end of extended track 'Overture'.

Joe had borrowed £150 ($195)

Cult DJ John Peel gave Def Leppard their first radio play.

> **"At first all we wanted to do was be successful in our home town."**
> *Rick Savage*

from his parents to pay for the session but they had to raise another £450 ($585) to press a thousand copies, this last money loaned from a friend—at a high rate of interest. The sleeve design featured a spoof on the His Master's Voice label (HMV) with a leopard instead of a dog and promotional copies of this ambitious EP were given away to friends and the rest mailed out to radio stations and magazines. They even managed to sell enough to make a profit!

Recalled Joe Elliott: "It was when we were all 17-years-old and still working during the day. We had a proper sleeve made with the leopard looking into a record player and with pictures on the back, credits, and lyric sheets. We sent copies off to the music papers and radio stations and sold a lot to friends. We sold about 900 copies in two weeks."

Rick Savage, Rick Allen, Steve Clark, Pete Willis and Joe Elliott in 1980

When they needed a name for their record label they remembered the abusive review they'd received for their gig at the Limit.

"They called us 'bludgeon riffola'—it was a complete slag off," said Joe. "So just to show that we didn't really care we picked up on the phrase and used it for the record label. The response to the EP was so spontaneous it was unbelievable, it actually got to Number 84 in the BBC chart—and this was without a record company! It created a great deal of interest and we got a two page spread in *Sounds* magazine."

The EP was picked up by local station Radio Hallam and the band recorded six songs for them. More importantly, when legendary British underground DJ John Peel visited Sheffield he was given a copy of the EP by Joe Elliott. Peel was a champion of alternative music and didn't have much time for heavy metal. But he liked the record, and told Joe to listen to his BBC Radio 1 show that night. He gave Def Leppard their first national airplay—1979 was proving to be an action-packed year for the band.

Radio plays

As the weeks went by their efforts triggered a shock wave that reverberated through the music industry. Almost overnight the bunch of school friends who had

Rick Allen joined Def Leppard at the age of 15

started out rehearsing and dreaming of stardom became one of the hottest bands in the country, and found themselves courted by the big guns of the industry.

With national publicity coming thick and fast the crowds at their gigs began to grow, and Def Leppard drew over 500 for a gig at Sheffield Polytechnic. What the audience saw was a band much improved on their spoon factory days and now powered by an excellent new drummer.

Before Frank Noon had deputized for them at the Hull studios, they'd asked if he'd like to stay on as a permanent fixture, but he refused out of loyalty to his own band. *The Sheffield Star* mentioned that Def Leppard were looking for a drummer in a story headed "Leppard Loses Skins". Word spread around town and reached the ears of 15-year-old wonder-drummer Rick Allen.

Rick contacted the band and they met at the Limit for an exploratory chat before the Leppards set off for Fairview to record with Frank Noon. Soon after those sessions Rick became the final piece in the Def Leppard jigsaw.

Born Richard John Cyril Allen on November 1, 1963, he was obsessed by drumming as a child. He built his own drum kit from biscuit tins and marched around the house. At the age of 11 he was given his first £60 ($78) drum kit and later took lessons—among his tutors was Kenny Slade who had

Sammy Hagar, who headlined Leppard's first London show in 1979.

33

AC/DC became big friends when Leppard supported them on tour.

played with Joe Cocker's Grease Band.

Rick formed his own band called Smokey Blue with a couple of friends on guitars, and later played with a much older rock band called Rampant. Now armed with a more professional drum kit, he began playing Deep Purple and Black Sabbath numbers. By the age of 13 he was a local celebrity on the semi-pro circuit and much in demand. He played with the Johnny Kalendar Band in working men's clubs when he was still at school and earned £10 ($20) a night.

Rick auditioned for Def Leppard the day after they finished their recording session and stunned the band with the power and precision of his playing. Rick, younger, yet already more experienced than any of the others, was the biggest boost since the arrival of Steve Clark.

Drum roll

They were now a tight, effective team ready to take on the world. At the last minute Tony Kenning hinted that he would like his old job back, but it was too late. Though still a schoolboy, Rick had become an official member of Def Leppard and his older brother Robert became the band's sound mixer and road manager.

The band were still rehearsing four hours a night, to perfect their stage act, but found themselves doing more and more live dates. Among the songs they were now

Hello America!

performing regularly were 'Glad I'm Alive', 'Rosalie', 'Ride Into The Sun', 'The Day The Walls Came Tumbling Down', 'Answer To The Master', 'The Overture', 'Good Morning Freedom', 'Wasted' and 'Getcha Rocks Off'.

It was all a far cry from the kind of stuff the Sex Pistols and the Clash were playing down in London. Asked why they didn't play punk, Joe Elliott replied bluntly: "Because we don't like it."

Added Rick Savage: "We're not

into punk. We were all heavy rock fans before we formed this band. I think the Pistols were brilliant, it's just that we all grew up on heavy rock and we're anxious to keep it going. If we did play punk we might disappear without a trace, because everybody's doing it aren't they?"

Rick Allen said he felt sick when he saw punk rockers pictured snarling in the music press.

"They try to look as horrible as possible. We're not like that. We try to look good and have style."

Rick Savage was even more forthright in his description of Def Leppard's aims and policies when he talked to *Sounds* reporter and early Leppard champion, Geoff Barton. Barton came from London to see the band play at Crookes Working Men's Club on June 5, 1979.

Rick Allen could be quite a trouble maker on tour.

Joe Elliott reaches for the sky.

"We're just doing what we want to do. Basically it's just down to the fact that we're all posers," admitted Rick cheerfully. "We all want to go out on stage, pose, wear dinky white boots, tight trousers and have all the girls looking at our bollocks. That's us. We like showing off, we're arrogant bastards, it's just like… over the top."

Sign here, please

The sudden rush of activity around the band had drawn them to the attention of two business men who became the group's first managers. Joe knew record retailer Peter Martin from visits to his Revolution Records store in Sheffield, which had been selling copies of *Getcha Rocks Off*. Discovering that the band didn't have a manager, Peter offered his services. He teamed up with Frank Stuart-Brown who was a promotion man for Arista Records and their new company MSB signed Def Leppard to a three-year management contract. The new managers took over the business side of the band from Joe and succeeded in getting *Getcha Rocks Off* played regularly on BBC Radio 1's Andy Peebles show.

The band, having sold 15,000 copies of the EP, now came to the attention of major record companies. The new managers ensured that when they played at the Porterhouse, Retford, on July 26, 1979, Leppard would be seen by both A&R men and rock critics. The following night the band played at the Rock Garden, Middlesbrough, where they were seen by Dave Bates from Phonogram—then a junior A&R man but later to become head of the department. Even though the sound system in the tiny club was rather poor, Bates was mightily impressed and couldn't believe how young the Leppards were. The record company folk were also relieved to see a band into solid, entertaining rock music, rather than just another bunch of angst-ridden punks into three discords and a drawn-out scream.

Even more importantly, an American A&R man was also interested. Cliff Burnstein, based at Mercury Records (part of Phonogram) in Chicago, had heard

Girl—the glam rock band who supported Def Leppard at 1980's Reading Festival.

> **"We grew up on heavy rock and we're anxious to keep it going. If we played punk we might disappear."**
> *Rick Savage*

Leppard developed a powerful stage show.

Getcha Rocks Off and was convinced that both fans and record buyers would like Def Leppard. He urged the British label to take them on board—and eventually Phonogram, in a deal negotiated by the band's managers, signed Def Leppard at Rick Allen's house where the band gathered on August 5. Because Rick was underage his father had to sign an extra clause in the contract on his behalf. As the pressure of work built up Rick had to leave school early and concentrate on his career.

Phonogram officially signed Bludgeon Riffola to Phonogram's Vertigo label and re-pressed *Getcha Rocks Off* which sold a further 24,000 copies. The next step was to start doing some recording for their parent company and the result was four songs—'Wasted', 'Rock Brigade', 'Hello America' and 'Glad I'm Alive'—recorded in London with producer Nick Tauber. The plan was to put out these as an EP but in the end 'Wasted' was released in September in single format and managed to get into the UK charts, peaking at Number 61. Unfortunately Cliff Burnstein didn't like the production of the song and ordered that the track shouldn't be released in America.

Going on tour

Meanwhile, the band's management had secured them a spot supporting American singer Sammy Hagar on four UK tour dates in September, which included their first appearance at the Hammersmith Odeon, London on the 16th. Among the numbers they played were 'Sorrow Is A Woman',

'Wasted' and 'Rock Brigade'.

Many of their old fans turned up to support them and, for the first time, heard material scheduled for their debut album. They also saw Joe Elliott wearing tight red pants and a T-shirt decorated with red hearts—a combination that caused a sensation among the girls.

Somebody else watching Leppard's lightning rise to fame was Peter Mensch. He was an astute

German heavy metallers the Scorpions welcomed Leppard on their US tour.

41

New York accountant and rock group manager working with the team of Leber and Krebs, who looked after bands like Aerosmith, Ted Nugent and Mahogany Rush. Mensch handled such luminaries of the hard rock stratosphere as AC/DC and the Scorpions. He was an associate of Cliff Burnstein and both went to see the band play at the Lafayette Club in Wolverhampton in September. Their plan was to take over management from Pete Martin and Frank Stuart-Brown to ensure Def Leppard would be handled properly on a world-wide basis.

The English managers set up a tour for the band supporting AC/DC, without realizing the deal was in fact the work of Burnstein and Mensch. It was great exposure

Reach out! Joe Elliott lost in the heat of the music.

for the Leppards and, apart from improving on their drinking skills with the Aussie band's singer Bon Scott, they also played to one of their biggest audiences—8,000—at the Bingley Hall, Stafford, on November 8. That was the same night that Peter Mensch offered to manage Def Leppard and, to add to the general favourable portents for the band's destiny, in the audience was their future producer, Robert John "Mutt" Lange, who had recently produced AC/DC's *Highway To Hell* album.

After discreet discussions with the band, the Americans took over and Leppard were signed to Leber and Krebs, from April 1, 1980 (Burnstein and Mensch would go on to form their own company, Q Prime, in 1982). The band's previous managers had to make do with royalty percentages from the early albums for Phonogram.

It was incredible to think that this exciting new band were attracting such interest and provoking cloak and dagger tactics from managers desperate to look after them when, just a few nights previously, on November 4 as they played another show at the Hammersmith Odeon, drummer Rick Allen was only just celebrating his 16th birthday!

Steve Clark in action with Def Leppard

Sunglasses and a cheeky Def Leppard grin

The London music papers were impressed by their performance and, backstage, Joe Elliott told one reporter his feelings about playing such a prestigious venue: "When we first played here with Sammy Hagar, it was the first time we'd been on a stage bigger than a postage stamp!" He admitted that he had got his microphone lead caught up around his ankles. "I've found it easier to get around the stage since I untied my ankles," he joked.

On a darker note, he revealed that

> **"When we played with Sammy Hagar it was the first time we'd been on a stage bigger than a postage stamp."**
> *Joe Elliott*

heavy touring was already beginning to wear out the young band.

Exhaustion sets in

"You are constantly wound up and it gets impossible to relax because you're worked up to a pitch of action. We're getting a rest after this tour to put down an album. We haven't had a chance to write much new material since all of this happened. We've been learning mainly about stage presentation. We haven't had the time to put a show together. All we do is go on and play the music. It's all very spontaneous."

Most of the songs in the bulk of their set were then 18 months old—the band knew they had to keep writing to sustain audiences and provide material for recording. Said Joe: "It doesn't really worry us. It just means that the writing is going to improve. Audiences are

45

Smoke gets in your eyes: Clark concentrates on his guitar.

listening to stuff that's a year old and it's going down well, so it can only get better."

By the autumn the band had already done two major UK tours. They had had to pay to play on their support slot for AC/DC, but they'd gained great exposure, and reached a total of 40,000 fans. In addition they had already experienced their first brushes with the superstars of rock. Joe told one reporter: "Sammy Hagar was a bit of a bighead—he never talked to us. But AC/DC are great. We have to be grateful to Hagar because he didn't short-change us and we got a fair deal out of him, but off-stage we feel a lot happier with AC/DC. They invited us back for a drink and everybody had a good laugh. Six months ago we'd never have dreamt of touring with these guys and there we were drinking with them."

Through the night

In November the band were voted fourth in the *Melody Maker*'s pop poll in the "Brightest Hope"

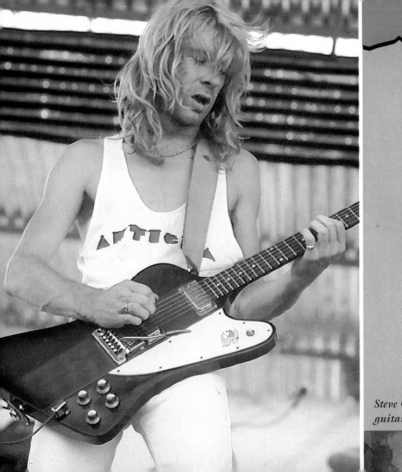

Steve Clark, lead guitarist

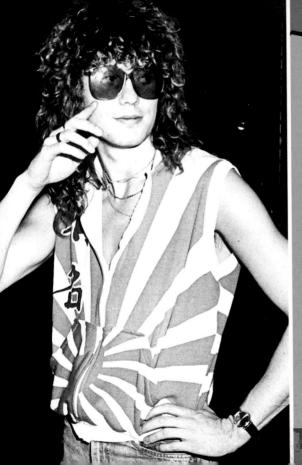

section, competing with the likes of the Pretenders and the Undertones.

After recording their first single the band went back to a studio in Ascot owned by Ringo Starr, to record their debut album *On Through The Night* with producer Tom Allom—who had worked with Judas Priest and Pat Travers. Astonishingly, most of the album was cut in a day, an indication of how familiar they were with the songs. They spent the rest of the time that had been booked doing over-dubs and remixes. Although, with hindsight, the album could have been brighter and doesn't now match up to Def Leppard's later work with Mutt Lange, there were some excellent performances featuring strong guitar work and powerful vocals—notably on

Rick Savage arriving for a show at the Los Angeles Forum, 1983.

Rick Allen

'Overture', 'Rock Brigade' and 'Wasted'. A new, stronger version of 'Hello America' was released as a single in February, 1980.

On Through The Night was released March 14, 1980, sold 30,000 copies and reached Number 15 in the UK Top 20 album chart. Consequently, more live work rolled in. They played at London's legendary rock venue, the Marquee Club—another dream fulfilled—and 50 other club dates around Britain.

Def Leppard had come a long way in a very short time. They were almost breathless with excitement as their rock fantasies literally came true. But they were already learning about the downside of the rock business—and the dangers. During the tour the band were shocked to hear of the death of their friend Bon Scott, the lead

singer with AC/DC, who was found dead in a car in London after a heavy drinking session. When the Leppards played a home-coming gig at Sheffield, they dedicated a song to Bon Scott's memory. AC/DC would return on fine form with Brian Johnson on vocals and the album *Back In Black*, but Scott's death was a warning to all rockers who over-indulged during their travels on the road.

Def Leppard's style of drinking had its roots in normal everyday social life in Sheffield. They had grown used to drinking in clubs and pubs from an early age. But for some of the band at least, now they had more time, more money and were under more pressure, drink was no longer mere recreation—it was becoming something more serious, the effects of which would soon be felt.

During March and April they played at bigger UK venues, including universities. They were gearing themselves up for their ultimate goal. In May, 1980, it was time to say "Hello America" for real! Excitement mounted as they headed for the land of opportunity and, unfortunately, Pete Willis became over excited and drank too much during the flight. The little lad from Sheffield, who had dreamed of taking America by storm in his college days, had to be carried off the plane unconscious when they arrived at Los Angeles.

Joe Elliott strains his throat.

> **"We've always been a prolific band. Writing good songs has never been a problem."**
> *Steve Clark*

HELLO AMERICA

America is the end of the rainbow as far as most aspiring British groups are concerned. Endless streams of young hopefuls set their sights on the US, desperate to emulate the worldwide success of bands like the Beatles, and Def Leppard were no exception—as the song 'Hello America' shamelessly confirmed. Their youthful good looks, energy and commitment to high-powered rock music ensured they would succeed, but America did not give in without a battle…

Their first US tour in May, 1980, comprised dates with Pat Travers, with the Scorpions and with Ted Nugent. The whole experience was a thrill for the band—but there was a peculiar backlash at home. One angry citizen of Sheffield actually wrote to the *Guardian*, one of Britain's quality national newspapers, to complain that Def Leppard had "sold out" by going abroad.

Joe Elliott reacted to this outbreak of provincialism with typical bluntness: "Selling out to America? That pisses me off because it's so ridiculous. We're not the first

> **"We've heard all this stuff about how our manager is manipulating us. Cobblers!"**
> *Joe Elliott*

English rock band to go to to the States and we won't be the last. You don't make money on tours in England. We're out to make Def Leppard a successful band and these days that means going to the States."

The band opened with 'Hello America' at their first American gig, supporting US band leader Pat Travers. They had a good reaction even though most of the audience had never heard of them. But after two weeks on tour the word began to spread and by the time they reached Portland, Oregon, the audience—including a high percentage of young girls—was on the side of this new sensation from the UK. Def Leppard blew Pat Travers off stage and 11,000 fans cheered them to the echo.

Soccer—Joe's second love

Black pvc pants and a Union Jack became Joe's uniform.

After the Travers gigs the band went out with English metal kings, Judas Priest, and in July played with Ted Nugent at several concerts— including one at a race track in Atlanta, Georgia. And on the night Joe Elliott celebrated his 21st birthday, they played at the Palladium, New York, supporting AC/DC once again. It was excellent exposure and helped them reach the hard core of America's rock fans.

As Leppard stormed around the States, they kept their stage act as tight as possible and avoided the usual kind of muso frills. This meant no long drum and guitar solos—a minimalism they had learned from the punk era. Rick Allen explained: "I enjoy doing solos but on this tour I've not had time to do one. The main aim is to get the band across. I can't be too upfront. We're not really a heavy metal band, we're more into melodic rock'n'roll and that's what they call it here in America—rock'n'roll!"

Added Pete Willis: "We had a really good time with Travers. Especially with Mars the bass player—he comes from Grimsby. We got really drunk together and on the last night with them it was crazy with custard pies thrown everywhere."

The management began to worry that the boys were drinking too much, too soon. And there was a problem with the youngest member. Rick, no stranger to trouble when at school, was now shooting his mouth off and getting stoned too often. But when word reached him that the organization

Off to America! Not bad for a young lad from Sheffield!

55

Jumping for joy—Steve Clark gets into the groove.

was actually considering giving him the sack, he calmed down. He wasn't the only one off the rails.

Pete Willis was also drinking, mainly to cover up his acute shyness and stage fright, but there wasn't much the band could do to stop him. It became the cause of increasing bad feeling between band members and Willis seemed to be turning into a liability.

In a bid to keep at least a partial grip on reality, the band took steps to keep fit, and began playing soccer during the day and swimming in the hotel pools to clear their heads in time for the nightly concerts. While the tour lost money because of the heavy cost of hotel and travel expenses, the exposure helped get them more airplay and album sales. *On Through The Night* peaked at

Number 51 in the Billboard Top 200 album chart.

Def Leppard were understandably delighted at the reaction they gained on this first American trip. The album had charted, they had played with all the top groups at the biggest venues, won a sizeable following and got rave reviews. Then they came home and got a bucket of cold water in the face .

Joe Elliott's jeans get frazzled on tour.

Goodbye England

In August the band returned to the UK for a special guest spot at the annual Reading Rock Festival in

> **"You'd be surprised how many records we've had to sell to pay our debts."**
> *Joe Elliott*

Maltese singer Marc Storace caused trouble when his band Krokus toured with Leppard.

Berkshire. There had already been a wave of anti-Leppard feeling among British heavy metal fans, and there were complaints in Sheffield that the band had been hyped, given too much money and had deserted their home town for America. Joe Elliott even got punched when he went back to one of his old drinking haunts. Their homecoming was an unpleasant experience, and it got to

be a lot worse when they appeared at Reading.

The 1980 bill included Iron Maiden, Whitesnake, UFO and Budgie. Def Leppard were scheduled to perform between Ozzy Osbourne and Whitesnake on the last night of three days. In the event Ozzy cancelled and was replaced at the last minute by Slade—a band that had enjoyed huge success among a young teenage audience in the early Seventies.

When it was their turn the compere said: "Let's hear it for Def Leppard!" "Boo!" came the answer from the crowd. "Boo!" It seemed unbelievable. The New Wave of British Heavy Metal was at a peak and here was an entertaining, all-British band who had been welcomed with open arms in the States. But this cut no ice with the greasers and bikers who had massed at the festival. Part of the problem

Portrait of a
guitarist: Steve
Clark

59

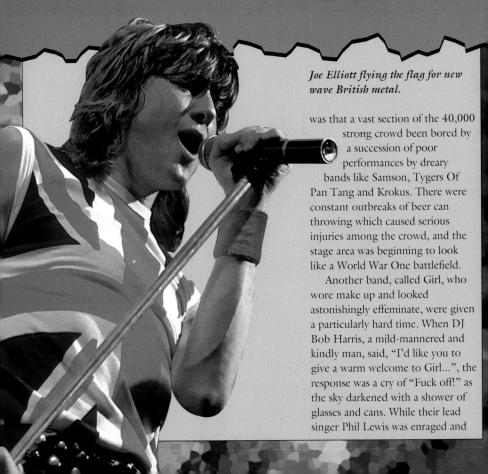

Joe Elliott flying the flag for new wave British metal.

was that a vast section of the 40,000 strong crowd been bored by a succession of poor performances by dreary bands like Samson, Tygers Of Pan Tang and Krokus. There were constant outbreaks of beer can throwing which caused serious injuries among the crowd, and the stage area was beginning to look like a World War One battlefield.

Another band, called Girl, who wore make up and looked astonishingly effeminate, were given a particularly hard time. When DJ Bob Harris, a mild-mannered and kindly man, said, "I'd like you to give a warm welcome to Girl...", the response was a cry of "Fuck off!" as the sky darkened with a shower of glasses and cans. While their lead singer Phil Lewis was enraged and their drummer was near to tears, their guitarist, Phil Collen, seemed more philosophical, despite the band going down badly. But he had no way of knowing at the time that in the not too distant future he would find himself no longer a Girl but a Def Leppard.

After this debacle the next band, Slade—old-timers from Wolverhampton—arrived, and it was obvious they knew exactly how to entertain a crowd. Their succession of chart hits like 'Cum On Feel The Noize' won them an ovation. They were going to be a tough act to follow.

Def Leppard climbed up the metal ramp to the stage. They were nervous but felt they shouldn't have much of a problem. They had to fare better than the tedious Tygers and be more appealing to the macho hordes than Girl. But there were loud groans at the very

mention of their name.

They played 'When The Walls Came Tumbling Down', 'Hello America' and 'Wasted', and they played them well. A huge video screen showed the boys in action,

Even Rick's playing couldn't save the band at the Reading Festival in 1980.

with Steve Clark bent over his guitar in agonies of concentration. A considerable section of the audience were impressed and cheers greeted 'Lady Strange'. But when Steve Clark pleaded with the crowd, "Let's hear some noise then", "Fuck off. We want Whitesnake", was all he got.

While the band escaped the ferocious canning off that Girl had suffered, they had their share of missiles. Joe was hit in the crotch with a full can of beer, a clod of turf crashlanded on Pete Willis' guitar and tomatoes and portions of half-consumed corn cobs fell on the stage at frequent intervals. It was pretty obvious that most of the crowd pressing up against the barriers were Whitesnake fans, and Def Leppard also suffered the disadvantage of not having a history

A study of Joe Elliott in blue jeans

was a picture of astonishment at the chorus of disapproval he received. Meanwhile, backstage, the band's manager Peter Mensch felt that they had suffered a serious setback and should concentrate on America where they were appreciated.

Joe looked back at the incident later and tried to work out what had actually happened.

"It's true we weren't that good, but there were a lot of things going against us. First there was just too much hard rock that weekend.

Rick Allen, the heavy heartbeat of Def Leppard

of chart hits behind them—only a reputation as brash newcomers. They went off—after an unwarranted encore—to a chorus of merciless boos.

Bob Harris came out all smiles, with another cheerful cry of "Let's hear it for Def Leppard". His face

"Selling out to America? That pisses me off. We're not the first English rock band that went to the States."
Joe Elliott

63

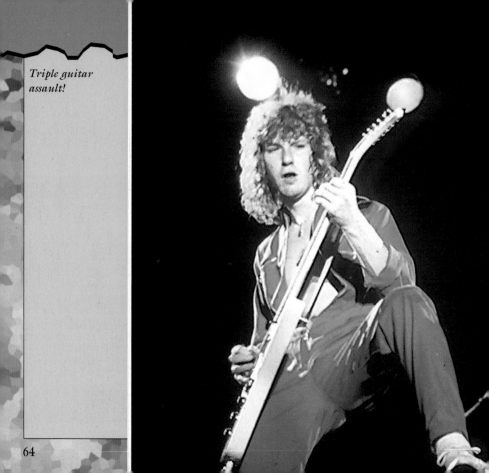

Triple guitar assault!

Every band seemed to be a hard rock band so there was no contrast. We were on on the last night and one of the last bands on the bill. I reckon anyone, even the most devoted fan of that kind of music, would get a bit fed up with it after three days, especially when you're sitting in a field being belted over the head with it. Probably the worst thing for us though was having to follow Slade. They were great. They put on an amazing show and went down a storm. They played all their hits and we didn't have any."

Flops and debts

Def Leppard escaped the Reading disaster to play some dates in Europe with the Scorpions, then in October quietly slipped back home to Sheffield to embark on a period of song writing. As their encouraging American debut slipped further into the rose-tinted past, it emerged that despite all their hard work and promising album sales the band were still in debt to their record company.

The only way forward was to record their second album, and they wanted the services of Mutt Lange as their producer. They had been after him for their first album, having heard his work with Seventies' artists City Boy, the Motors and Graham Parker.

"Our first producer Tom Allom was great, but we didn't want to use him on the second album," explained Joe. "We didn't want to get stuck in a rut. We wanted it to be a definite improvement."

Mutt was busy working with Foreigner on their fourth album, so Def Leppard had to wait a few months. Joe Elliott, against Steve

Joe Elliott: rock god

Ritchie Sambora from Bon Jovi gets friendly with Joe Elliott.

Clark's wishes, decided they should do a short club tour in December 1980 to prove to the fans that they hadn't been deserted. But attendances were poor and only 87 fans came to see them at Nottingham's Beat Club where, a year earlier, they had packed the place and 400 fans had been turned away. Only 150 came to see them at the Retford Porterhouse and they had to cancel Doncaster when they sold only three advance tickets! When they played Dunstable, Bedfordshire, they did draw a better crowd but their performance was poor. Among the audience was Phil Collen, the guitarist from Girl.

When Pete Willis' gear broke down, it was Phil rushed on to help Pete change his guitar. He would soon be seeing a lot more of the Leppard stage.

It seemed the band were now in serious danger of sliding down the slippery slope they thought they had conquered, and a return to obscurity beckoned ominously. In June 1981 they went on a European tour supporting Ritchie Blackmore's Rainbow—but, under-rehearsed, by the time they arrived for the first gig in Germany, Joe had worn his voice out singing in the studio on tracks for their new album—aptly titled *High'n'Dry*.

High'n'Dry

Technically this was a much better production than *On Through The Night* and also included a new Leppard ballad—'Bringing On The Heart Break'.

> ## "Mutt Lange is a slave driver, but he is a genius."
> *Steve Clark*

69

Joe Elliott sang the praises of Lange when he said that: "Mutt is an excellent producer. I think we are going to surprise a lot of people who thought we were just a flash in the pan." Steve Clark agreed.

"The guy is a slave driver but he's a genius."

With such a powerful producer and astute management behind them, it was rumoured that Def Leppard were just pawns in the hands of the rock industry, a slur the band deeply resented. After all, they had built themselves up from nothing by their own efforts.

"We've heard all that stuff about how our manager is manipulating us and how we are playthings of our record company," declared Joe hotly. "Cobblers! We have a say in what records come out and what tours we do, and as far as our music is concerned that's completely down to us. We're not a bunch of idiots who don't know how to make a decision. We've got minds of our own and we know how to use them."

The new album sold around 200,000 in its first weeks of release in America, but the tracks didn't get as much airplay as expected. Many felt the music was becoming too sophisticated and it actually sold less copies in the UK than the first album. Joe later admitted it could have been better.

"The results were something of a mess. It wasn't really a bad album but it didn't capitalize on our strengths. *Pyromania* was our real second album."

Def Leppard once more trotted off on a short headlining tour of the UK in July but again attendances and reviews were poor. It was almost a relief to fly back to America where they supported Ozzy Osbourne and a Southern boogie

Bryan Adams, also produced by Mutt Lange, meets Joe Elliott.

band called Blackfoot. The tour was full of dramatic incidents, with property stolen, promoters refusing to pay up and tensions rising between the exhausted band members. But if nothing else, at least the album was beginning to do better and the band were regularly blowing Blackfoot off-stage—the American band gave in eventually and asked Leppard to headline.

Drinks all round

In November the newly launched and increasingly influential all-music US cable video channel MTV discovered the band's video for 'Bringing On The Heartbreak' and began to give it healthy amounts of exposure, pushing the album back up the charts. In September it reached Number 38 in the US charts, while in Britain it peaked at Number 26.

After the setbacks in Europe it

Getting their rocks off on stage.

seemed that the boys were on the verge of achieving a real breakthrough. But behind the scenes tension was mounting once again. Both Steve Clark and Pete Willis responded to the pressures of heavy touring by turning to drink, and Joe Elliott was understandably cross. He would try to lecture Pete, only to incur the wrath of Rick Savage who tried to look after his old mate. The result was an outbreak of hostilities between Joe and Rick. Willis began to consider leaving the band.

They returned to Europe to play a dozen or so dates with Judas Priest. The band had been on the road for months and, desperate to get back home, they weren't too upset when the German part of the tour was cancelled. At the beginning of 1982 the band found some comfort in learning that *High'n'Dry* had sold more than *On Through The Night*, but it sometimes seemed that their rock'n'roll dreams were turning into a nightmare. What they needed was a big hit album and a lot of hit singles—and soon.

In January 1982 they began work on the third album—one they were determined would bring international stardom and set standards for future rock albums. It was the result of weeks of hard work in the studios, under the tutelage of Mutt Lange. The South African-born producer who had done such wonders for AC/DC liked Def Leppard for their zest, enthusiasm and ideas, and was impressed by their use of original riffs and Queen-like harmonies. He helped them get their ideas onto record by showing Joe how to sing more efficiently, and by explaining to the rest of the band how to make use of dynamics by not playing everything at full speed and volume. It was hard work for everyone and a million miles from jamming in a rehearsal room. Tempers became frayed to the point of fights between band members—but it was worthwhile in the end.

Pyromania was about to set the world on fire.

> *"A lot of bands stopped thinking about the music and lived a silly lifestyle. We're not pompous. We're very sincere. We don't live in mansions."*
> *Phil Collen*

73

PYROMANIA!

During 1982 the first major split occurred within the ranks of Def Leppard. They had been through various drummers in their early stages, but none of the founder members had been dropped. The dismissal of erring guitarist Pete Willis would be a painful decision, but it had to be made—for all their sakes.

Relations had become increasingly fraught during the 1981 US tour with Blackfoot, and there were further problems during the recording of *Pyromania*. Pete's drinking made him increasingly unreliable and difficult to handle. He could no longer cope with the rigours of touring and its attendant excesses. He missed several recording sessions and provided a

variety of unacceptable excuses. It came to a head one morning when he arrived at the studio to record a solo for a track called, appropriately enough in his case, 'Stagefright'.

Although it was early in the day there was no mistaking the fact he was drunk, despire his best attempts

Bruce Dickinson (right) of Iron Maiden, with Joe at MTV's European launch

to conceal it from Mutt Lange. He could barely hit the strings of his guitar, let alone the right notes. The producer angrily ordered him out of the studio, told him to go home and not return until he could play properly. Ashamed and expecting the worst, Pete Willis departed—never to play with Def Leppard again.

Fired!

On July 11, 1982, he was formally ordered out of the band. Joe Elliott had the task of telling him in a phone call to Willis' home, but the guitarist insisted on coming down to see the band at a meeting in London. When it was finally made plain he could no longer be in the band, he accepted the decision and was relieved it was all over.

The lead guitarist from Girl, Phil Collen, had shared the bill with them at the Reading Festival and was already a friend of the band, having sat in with them on several

Def Leppard in their good-lookin', hard-rockin' prime

occasions. The band were happy to welcome him into the fold. Affable, good looking and a fine musician, he was the only one they wanted to replace Willis.

Phil was given tapes from the uncompleted *Pyromania* sessions and asked to devise some solo ideas. He went to Battery studios, met Mutt Lange, played his solos, and was immediately accepted as a full member of Def Leppard. Phil featured on some of the major cuts on the new album including 'Rock Of Ages', 'Photograph', 'Foolin' and 'Rock! Rock! (Till You Drop)'. He was also able to contribute backing vocals and rhythm guitar and he proved a steady partner for Steve Clark.

"When Phil turned up it was a great kick up the ass for me…" said

Steve. "It provided me with some really good competition. I had probably got into a bit of a rut. When Phil joined it was a completely fresh attitude."

Joe told how Pete had soured the atmosphere in Leppard before his departure: "He used to get kinda funny on us sometimes. But he was having personal problems and they were screwing him up. He turned to drink and the result was he played too slow and became very moody. He was always a bit of a beast on tour and he was getting like an animal in the studio too. We decided it would be better if he left the band. Things came to a head in the studio and it became clear that we couldn't go on as we were. I tried my bloody hardest to get on with Pete but we just drifted aeons apart. We had known Phil for ages. We always kept in touch and respected him as a guitarist. We knew he would work hard. He also had the right looks for our group. We wasted little time getting hold of him once we realized it wasn't going to work anymore with Pete."

Pyromania unleashed

Work continued on the album for virtually the whole of 1982 and it was finally released, along with a single 'Photograph', in January 1983. This third album from Def Leppard caused a sensation that

New kid on the block Phil Collen gets down to work.

went far beyond the narrow confines of the NWOBHM. The brilliant production, the riff-laden tunes, clever hook lines, vocal harmonies, and blasting drum sound competed with the best that the advanced techno-pop of the day could offer, while retaining the spirit of a traditional rock group.

America loved the whole concept. At long last the British were sending them something they could appreciate, a band whose music could be translated into record and ticket sales, radio plays and MTV video "heavy rotation". Def Leppard delivered youth rock music for the Eighties and they were welcomed with open arms. Although the band had been deep in debt, all the signs were that riches lay ahead.

From February onwards *Pyromania* began a 92-week run in the US charts, spending two weeks at Number 2 and only held off the top spot by the irresistible force of Michael Jackson's blockbuster *Thriller*. In March the album reached Number 18 in the UK Top 20 and the group began a series of British dates which were to be the first part of a massive world tour. For most of the year the album sold at a steady 100,000 copies a week and eventually sold seven million copies in the US. It was a phenomenal reaction, and a tribute to Mutt Lange and the band's painstaking work. It was also a wonderful introduction to Leppard

> ## "We expect better things for the future now that Phil Collen is in the group."
> *Rick Savage*

Happy days when **Pyromania** *ruled the world*

Back to basics life for Phil Collen.

But while the band's star was in the ascendancy, their previous guitar player became a recluse in Sheffield. Pete Willis' life was made even sadder by the death of his mother from a heart attack. He would later form his own groups without much success, but managed to survive on royalties from Leppard.

The group played a warm-up date at London's Marquee Club on February 9, 1983, to get Phil Collen used to being a "live" Leppard. The club was packed to the doors and the band found one of their early idols becoming a friend as guitarist Brian Robertson, of Thin Lizzy fame, sat in with them there.

Next stop was a "Rock Till You Drop" British tour that once again proved the public at home were playing hard to get. Apart from one show at Sheffield City Hall none of the dates were sell-outs. However their date in Belfast on the 11th caused a sensation among the rock-starved hordes, and Def Leppard created as much excitement in the city as Led Zeppelin had done some ten years earlier.

By the time Leppard returned to London's Hammersmith Odeon on March 4 they had already been to France, Holland, Belgium and all around England. They took London by storm and delivered a blistering performance that erased any lingering memories of their Reading Festival debacle. They exuded confidence and power. The audience leapt to their feet and stayed there throughout a show which was a non-stop assault on eyes and ears.

Fans held blazing cigarette lighters aloft for the slow ballads and shook their hair in true headbangers' style for the rockers. Although the band looked young and flashier than ever, they performed like seasoned pros, and made full use of special lighting effects, smoke, flames and explosions. Joe Elliott, muscles rippling, clad in black PVC trousers covered in studs, chains, belts and padlocks, sang with a uniquely passionate intensity.

It was probably the Odeon show

Leppard on the prowl

that finally convinced the British rock press Leppard should be taken seriously and that Elliott was a singer of merit. Here was a new idol set to follow in the footsteps of old-timers Robert Plant and Ian Gillan. Joe ripped off his jacket revealing a Union Jack waistcoat, while his cohorts, all skinny legs and long hair, danced around each other in a frenzied guitarists' ballet.

Fuelled with adrenaline, Elliott jumped onto the lighting rig to turn a spotlight onto the audience, then launched into 'Photograph'. It was a performance which highlighted Phil Collen's speedy guitar work, Joe introducing Collen to the crowd with a jokey: "He used to be a Girl—but he got better."

It was inevitable that at some point Elliot would yell: "London, are you with us—we want to hear you make some noise!", but this time there was none of the rejection they'd suffered at Reading. The anthemic 'Rock Of Ages' had the audience chanting along to the chorus with Elliott and Rick Savage. 'Bringin' On The Heartbreak' brought the show to a blazing climax.

Def Leppard achieved their

> ## "Deep down inside, we'd love to be big in Britain. It's a matter of pride."
> *Joe Elliott*

major American breakthrough that same year, 1983. In May, 'Photograph' reached Number 12 in the US charts and in August 'Rock Of Ages' went to Number 16 (the song also reached Number 41 in the UK singles chart).

Rock'n'roll dreams

The guys went back to America to support Billy Squier and his band after the spring tour of the UK and Europe. On their opening night of March 18 in Atlanta, Georgia, a nervous Phil Collen made his American debut and passed with flying colours. In April the band

Phil and Joe give the audience what they want.

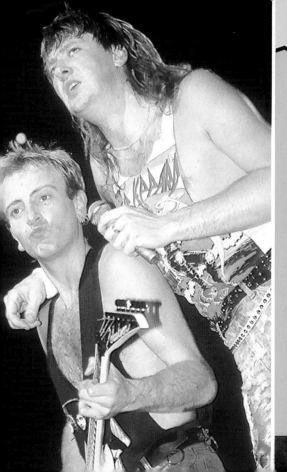

went out on their first headlining dates in the States, starting on April 30 in Odessa, Texas. The strength of their appeal to a massive young audience took doubting promoters by surprise.

Rock music in the mid-Eighties had been undergoing one of its periodic crises. As bands get older, their audience matures and begins to identify other priorities—like getting married and buying a home. Soon concert attendance figures drop as a previous hot ticket becomes less of an attraction.

Now Def Leppard had arrived to invigorate the US concert season. They drew a new audience of young girls who had previously ignored all forms of old-time rock with its contingent of beer-gutted, balding anti-heroes. Def Leppard's sexy good looks changed all that. One fan was heard crying after a show, "they look just like little toy dolls.

83

They're so sweet".

The band were greeted with screaming hysteria whenever they showed their faces, whether it was in a hotel lobby or at record signing sessions. Girls mobbed and chased them, so much so that the band had to use decoys, and even disguise themselves, if they wanted to venture out into the street.

Blitzing the world: Leppardmania began to take off in 1983.

As they charged around the States, supported by bands like Krokus, Gary Moore and the Jon Butcher Axis, everyone wanted a piece of the action. Rock celebrities rang demanding backstage passes and even the late Frank Zappa asked if he could get Leppard tickets for his son Dweezil.

Other stars weren't content with

just watching the action. While rock legendaries Queen were taking a break from their schedule, guitarist Brian May went on holiday in America, producing Scottish group Heavy Pettin' who told him about Leppard's success and music.

He offered to sit in and play guitar with the young melodic rockers, jamming with them on the John Fogerty song 'Travellin' Band' that had become one of their favourites. For the band his presence was the highlight of two sell-out shows at the Los Angeles Forum in September and the start of a friendly association between Leppard and Queen: after sitting in with them, May was a Leppard convert.

The Queen's favourites

"I was bowled over by them. They were just amazing. Their show was one of the highest energy things I had ever seen. They destroyed the place. I went backstage and told 'em so, and they invited me to play with them the next night. I was highly flattered so I went on and played a song at the end of the show, which was great fun."

The event was watched by a crowd of 16,000. Among them were the band's parents, flown out

Joe shows Phil how to play guitar in 1983.

85

Buddies—Steve Clark and Joe Elliott in 1983

expert, nick-named Pyro Pete. They also saw Joe Elliott, clad in a Union Jack tee shirt and leather pants, leaping from the PA stack to the lighting rig in an exuberant display of athletic prowess. To show solidarity with American fans, Joe even stripped off his Union flag top to reveal a Stars and Stripes T-shirt underneath.

The Union flag theme was extended to pairs of shorts worn by the band on endless photo sessions and sold to fans in a flow of merchandise. Tickets and T-shirts alone brought in around $15 million (£11.5 million) during the tour. Superficially, it seemed like a bonanza, but in reality it was a fair reward for four years of hard work and accumulated debt. They had to sell a lot of records to become solvent. While many observers now thought the Sheffield lads were all millionaires, Joe Elliott explained

especially from Sheffield to LA to see the unbelievable extent of their boys' success. They saw a show packed with explosions, sheets of flame and giant Catherine Wheels, the latter set off during 'Rock Of Ages' by the band's special effects

the truth of the situation.

Phil Collen sings.

"The band is a millionaire. We as individuals aren't. Compared to what we're used to, we are gonna be bloody rich. But I'm not embarrassed about it at all—we've earned every penny. We have slogged our guts out for years and it's taken its toll."

Apathy in the UK

Pyromania sales continued to escalate. The album turned platinum in Canada and by July it had sold five million in the States. Yet back home in England it had

> *"Joining Def Leppard offered no real problems. I'd jammed with them in the past."*
> *Phil Collen*

barely sold 30,000: it was reported that they sold five times as many copies of *Pyromania* in Seattle as they did in the UK, and the total British sales of all three Leppard albums didn't even match up to one week's sales of *Pyromania* in the States. They even sold more US concert tickets than they sold UK albums during their triumphant progress around America in 1983, when they were playing to 15,000 people a night. One concert, at the Jack Murphy Stadium in San Diego, drew 55,000 to see Def Leppard topping a bill that included guitarist Eddie Money, prog-rock monsters Uriah Heep, and hard rockers Motley Crüe. But the continued lack of interest at home was a source of hurt and indignation.

"Deep down inside we'd love to be big in Britain. It's a matter of pride. We wanna be big at home," revealed Joe Elliot. "If we didn't care, we wouldn't even bother playing in England." When they did play at home, it was usually at a high cost. It was estimated that their UK spring tour that year lost them £50,000 (about $85,000).

In America, Def Leppard got on well with their support acts most of the time and tried to treat them fairly, but there were difficult moments. An unnecessary feud developed with Swiss rockers

> **"We've always had a plan for success. From the very start we've known what we wanted to accomplish. Everything's progressed amazingly."**
> *Joe Elliott*

Phil Collen, the new boy who became a Leppard veteran.

Krokus, who were fronted by an ambitious Maltese singer called Marc Storace. He had committed the cardinal sin of copying Joe's stage act, stealing lines of dialogue Joe normally used to address the audience, and aping his climbing-over-the-PA-speakers routine.

The singer had been told he shouldn't climb the Leppard's scaffolding towers or special steps up to the PA, but he broke the rules on the first night of the tour. Another support act advised Joe he should go out and see what Storace was doing during Krokus' set.

"I went out to watch them from the side of the stage, and I couldn't believe my ears", fumed Elliott. "Marc Storace was saying every single line I'd said the night before, so when I came out with them an hour later they fell flat."

Krokus were given a warning and there was a row backstage involving both bands and their managers. The Swiss band complained they had been denied proper facilities for their act.

"I don't know what the band's problem was," said Joe Elliott later. Eventually Krokus left the tour, still vehemently protesting, and claiming they were "too hot to handle".

There were more important problems to cope with. Joe's voice began to suffer and he had to see a specialist to advise him on how to sing and breathe correctly. Humidity and air conditioning did not help and because of the strain of heavy touring they had to cancel eight shows. He began to take a humidifier around with him to lubricate his throat.

The Leppard circus continued to criss-cross the States, eventually reaching San Francisco where US rockers Journey turned out to watch them. Then towards the end of the year Def Leppard returned for an eventful jaunt in Europe.

Big in Japan

In Geneva Swiss fans let off their own pyro display—sparks from the audience set off the band's special

Phil Collen, lead guitarist with Girl, replaced Pete Willis in Leppard.

but got up and chased his assailant into the crowd. There was a full-scale fight between Joe and his roadies and a gang of thugs. The show had to be cut short.

After sell-out shows in Paris, France, Def Leppard returned to England to play in Birmingham and once again at the Hammersmith Odeon, London, on December 5. This time the British shows were sell-outs but the tour wasn't over yet. With demand for their services at an all-time high, they went off to Japan, Australia and Thailand in the New Year before finally coming home to rest and recover in February 1984.

Phil Collen had experienced an extraordinary baptism by fire but still claimed: "It's been the best year of my life—without doubt." However, his frontman Joe Elliott had been riding the Leppard juggernaut for some years and could

Def Leppard on the couch

effects too soon and the boys had to flee the stage. In San Sebastian, Spain, a coin was thrown which hit Joe Elliott in the face and just missed his eye. He fell to the floor,

be forgiven for feeling overwrought and nostalgic .

"Five years ago I was driving a van," he said on his return to Sheffield. "Now I'm only allowed into Britain for 62 days a year unless I want to hand over 80 per cent of my money in tax—which I don't. Who would have thought it?"

The popularity of the band, especially in America, could be gauged by the results of the 1983 Readers' Poll in the influential *Circus* magazine. Out of 11 possible awards the band and their producer Mutt Lange won eight. They were voted Best Group and Best In Concert Group. They received the Best Video award, Joe was Best Male Vocalist (beating Robert Plant), and *Pyromania* was Best Album. Mutt Lange was Best Producer, and Rick Allen was Best Drummer. Steve Clark was only pipped to the post of Best Guitarist

Joe Elliott relaxes on the road.

by Eddie Van Halen. They went on to win even more awards in a whole range of music magazines as Leppard fans swamped the postal services with their votes.

The boys were suitably humbled by these accolades.

"It's very kind of everybody. But as far as I'm concerned I can't hold a candle to someone like Robert Plant," believed Joe Elliott. "I have improved over the past few years but I'm still not as good as I want to be."

1992 o music awards

As 1984 loomed, the main priority was to find a follow-up to *Pyromania*. This was likely to involve a lot of work, but it was achievable—the future looked bright and carefree. Def Leppard need only consolidate their hard-won success. All they had to do was make music and have more fun together. None of the band or their management, friends and fans could foresee the tragic events that lay ahead.

The MTV Music Awards would provide awards for the boys within a few years.

"A lot of people out there still really like us. We've never tried to be political and we've always tried to make escapist rock music."

Phil Collen

BRINGIN' ON THE HEARTBREAK

Def Leppard were on top of the world at the beginning of 1984. They were one of the few British rock bands in years to have achieved palpable international success. Their records had the dynamic power to lift heavy rock into a new era and, as a concert attraction, they had won over a new young audience. Critics might sneer at "macho posing" and decry the studio wizardry employed to create *Pyromania* but there was no doubting the scale of their triumph. All they required now was inspiration to keep the music flowing and strength to keep up the momentum.

On February 7 their world tour

Def Leppard reveal a garish dress sense at a Nordoff Robbins charity lunch.

had ended in Bangkok where they played to 6,000 fans. Dublin was the next stop, to rest, recuperate, escape punitive UK income tax and think about the future.

Writing and recording sessions began there in May. Each member of the band was armed with a drum machine to help them work on song ideas for the fourth album. The problem was, Mutt Lange no longer wanted to produce them. He was exhausted after completing an album with American band the Cars. He assured the band they could do the next one without him.

Talks went ahead with other producers and in August sessions began at Wisseloord Studios, Hilversum, Holland, with producer/writer Jim Steinman—who had worked on Meatloaf's *Bat Out Of Hell* blockbuster. Alas, by November it became apparent that Jim's style was incompatible with the band's, and some eight tracks had to be scrapped. Jim was replaced by Nigel Green who had engineered *High'n'Dry*. During the delay the record company put out a revamped version of that album in America, including a re-mixed version of 'Bringin' On The Heartbreak'—also issued as a single which peaked at 61 in the US charts. A special video of the song was shot in Dublin with director David Mallet.

Video power

While the band were contemplating their future, it was also a time to pause and reflect. Rick Allen explained: "At first all we wanted to do was be successful in our home town. Then we wanted to tour Britain. When we saw that those goals were within our reach we

> **"The band is a millionaire. We as individuals aren't."**
> *Joe Elliott*

began to think about America. When we had a chance to be the opening act there for AC/DC it was like fulfilling our wildest dream. When we were able to play to huge crowds all around the country it was the most incredible experience of our lives."

"We couldn't believe there were so many people who were into our music," added Rick Savage. "We'd play in front of 20,000 fans one night, drive to the next town and there would be 20,000 more screaming just as loud."

A crucial factor in the band's breakthrough was the use of videos. Thanks to MTV millions of Americans saw the band storming through 'Photograph', 'Rock Of Ages' and 'Foolin' on action-packed promos beamed into their homes.

"We enjoyed an incredible response when we did the video for 'Bringin' On The Heartbreak'," said Steve Clarke. "We did it a couple of months after the album had been released and it perked up sales. We really enjoyed making them—each video had a different theme and we did them all at one time over the span of a couple of days. Our music stands up on its own, but the video adds an extra element."

Joe Elliott spelt out the band's goals: "We're conscious about doing something that's original rather than just mimicking. We understand the traditions of rock'n'roll because we're still fans as well as musicians. We have tried to create music that's powerful but also has melodic hooks. We're not out there to blow people away, like Mötorhead. We want to perform songs that people appreciate for their musical quality as well as for their energy. We always had confidence in ourselves. But I must admit, even we were a little

Unmistakeably Leppard? They were once called "a German heavy metal trio"!

surprised by the degree of attention we received. We always felt we'd eventually be successful because we're not scared to work hard. We always had a plan for success. From the very start we've known what we wanted to accomplish and while we were side-tracked at the beginning of our career, we got straightened out and everything progressed amazingly well."

The crash

As Christmas 1984 loomed, the band took a rest from their recording sessions in Holland and

Rick Allen was to suffer a horrific car crash in 1984, but would continue playing.

returned to England for the holiday. It was time for fun and relaxation.

On New Year's Eve Rick Allen and his girlfriend Miriam Barendsen went out for an afternoon drive in his brand new Corvette Stingray. Unfortunately, the sight of the young couple passing by at speed in an expensive sports car enraged two men in an Alfa Romeo. They decided to pass the Stingray on a

bridge and then to slow down in front of the American car—just to cause maximum irritation.

When Rick tried to pass, the Alfa driver began to force him off the road. As the Stingray accelerated, Rick was faced with a left hand bend which he failed to negotiate. The car hit a brick wall and turned over on its roof. The other car drove off, leaving Miriam trapped in the wreck. Rick Allen was thrown free into a field, but his left arm was ripped off at the shoulder.

Within minutes of the accident two nurses, one who lived nearby and another in a passing car, came to the rescue. They bandaged Rick's wounds and packed the severed arm in ice while waiting for an ambulance. Rick and Miriam were taken to the Royal Hallamshire Hospital in Sheffield. When they heard the news, the band broke down in tears.

Miriam had suffered head injuries and bruising but later made a full recovery. However, Rick underwent a four-hour operation during which a top surgeon attempted to sew back his arm. Unfortunately it failed—the limb had become infected and had to be removed.

A few days later the band decided to meet up again in Holland and start recording again. Rick's drum parts had already been done. They felt it was better to carry on in hope, rather than sit around doing nothing.

Expressions of sympathy came in from all over the world, particularly from fellow drummers. However, there were others who couldn't wait to apply for the "vacant job" of drummer with Def Leppard. Their calls were greeted with contempt. They hadn't reckoned on the resolve of the band—and of their

> **"As far as England is concerned, people have got something against Def Leppard for non-musical reasons."**
> *Joe Elliott*

21-year-old drummer.

In the weeks after the accident Rick decided he had to face the world rather than sit at home. He wanted to be with his old friends so, not long out of hospital, he flew to Holland to meet the band and confirm that he wanted to stay on—somehow. He began a long process of physical and mental recovery, fighting off fits of depression with the support of friends and family.

In fact within 18 months he was back on stage with them, playing a specially-adapted electronic drum kit. Despite the accident, he and the band were able to enjoy a new lease of life and hope.

"When the rest of the guys in the band started visiting me and giving me the kind of encouragement that I really needed, I realized there was a way I could play again," said Rick

Recording during 1985 was slow and arduous. Tapes were made and scrapped. Rick Allen began to learn how to play a custom-built Simmons electronic drum kit, fitted with foot pedals to enable him to produce the beats he would normally have used his left arm to play. He also used a computer to store various drum sounds for use in the studio. Rick spent many frustrating hours trying to perfect a new drumming technique, but he was given full encouragement by the band.

The beat goes on

By mid-summer the band had their fourth album more or less complete. But when Mutt Lange heard it, he decided it needed re-working. He promised to help them out, but it would mean spending another year in the studio.

The band hoped to tour, using drummer Jeff Rich from Status Quo to supplement Rick Allen's work on the electronic kit. But the return to

Def Leppard—getting to the top of the rock tree.

most of the show by himself. That's when the band realized—Rick could do it all on his own. Jeff Rich said goodbye and Def Leppard had their regular drummer back again.

Hysteria breaks out

Rick's first major assignment with the new set-up came when they were booked to play at the 1986 Monsters Of Rock festival at Castle Donington, England, and at two other heavy metal festivals in Sweden and Germany. The crowds' heartwarming welcome encouraged Rick to carry on with his playing career. And the reception also gave added impetus to efforts to produce a worthy follow-up to *Pyromania*.

But Leppard's run of bad luck hadn't finished. When they played the final 'Monsters' show at Mannheim, Germany, on August 31, there was a torrential downpour of rain that lasted throughout the

the studio meant they couldn't contemplate going back on the road. Their first appearance since Rick's accident came in August 1986 when they played some small warm-up gigs in Ireland during which Rick got used to playing on stage again, helped out by Jeff Rich.

When Jeff was late arriving at a gig one night, Rick had to play

103

Steve caught in a moody shot.

entire set. They were all soaked and risked electrocution but refused to stop playing. Later in November Joe Elliott became ill with an attack of mumps, and then in December Mutt Lange was injured in a car crash on the way to Wisseloord studios and spent three weeks in hospital with leg injuries.

Despite all these setbacks, work continued on the album and one extraordinary arrangement, the tense and dramatic 'Pour Some Sugar On Me', later became one of the hottest numbers on the new album—eventually called *Hysteria*.

Although it took nearly three years to get the album organized, the tracks that made it onto the final record were cut in just a few days in February 1987. Highlights were 'Armageddon It', 'Women', 'Rocket', 'Animal', 'Love Bites',

'Gods Of War', 'Don't Shoot', 'Shot Gun', 'Run Riot', 'Hysteria', 'Excitable' and 'Love And Affection'. While Mutt Lange spent a further two months at his mixing desk, the band geared themselves up for a year of interviews, promotion and a return to touring.

The first single from the album, 'Animal', was released in the summer and peaked in the UK Top 20 at Number 6. *Hysteria* was put out on August 29, 1987, and went straight in at UK Number 1, spending 95 weeks in the UK charts. In October 'Pour Some Sugar On Me' reached Number 18 in the UK, and 'Hysteria',

Facing the press, their fans and another hotel bill.

Steve Clark, with escort, at the MTV Awards in LA in 1989

'Armageddon It', 'Love Bites' and 'Rocket' were all hits as well. At long last it was incontrovertibly demonstrated that, not before time, Def Leppard were stars in their own country—*Hysteria* eventually sold some 15 million copies, including ten million in America.

In September 1987 the band began a new world tour, with Rick Allen firmly in charge on the drums. In America they decided to use a concert presentation technique, playing in the round with their stage set in the centre of arenas, to allow everyone in the audience a closer glimpse of their heroes. The tour was a huge success and hits flooded out on both sides of the Atlantic.

'Pour Some Sugar On Me' went to Number 2 in the US Top 100 of July 1988 but celebrations were muted—one of the band's roadies, Steve Cayter, had died of a brain haemorrhage on stage just before a show at the Alpine Valley Music Theatre, Wisconsin. But by now the unstoppable Leppard machine had more than enough momentum to carry on positively and with more success stories.

At the start of the following year, the band started writing songs for their next album. In February they performed live at the eighth annual BRIT Awards held at London's Royal Albert Hall, and then at the annual MTV Video Awards at the Universal Amphitheatre, Los Angeles, in September.

A death in the family

Then things went strangely quiet. The band mysteriously disappeared from view during 1990, taking the

Rick Savage gets down to bassics.

Vivian Campbell stepped in after Steve Clark's tragic death in 1990.

whole of the summer off. An ominous sign—it indeed transpired that they had been undergoing another crisis, which finally came to a head on January 8, 1991 when the rock world was shocked to hear of the death of their guitarist Steve Clark. He had been out for a night's drinking with a friend and his body was found by his girlfriend the next morning in his Chelsea flat in London. His death was caused by an accidental combination of alcohol, anti-depressants and some pain-killers he had been taking for three cracked ribs.

It was revealed later that the 30-year-old Clark had been suffering from alcoholism and depression, a condition not alleviated by his band's fame and fortune. In fact he had been an alcoholic since the age of 18, when he was still working in a factory back in Sheffield.

"He was a shy, ordinary guy, though on stage he had a magnetic presence. He looked like a rock star, much more so than anybody else in the band. But he was the most normal out of the lot of us. We had been through a lot of times together, good, bad and indifferent. We grew up and matured together," said devastated Joe Elliott. "As a band we all had our distractions, whether it was families, videos or soccer. Steve had a guitar and he had a bottle…. they were the only two things in his life. It was difficult because he was an alcoholic and he had a lot of problems. We spent a long time trying to pull him out of that because he was our friend. We told him he was killing himself, but he didn't believe us. We miss him and we always will. Thank God he left something behind that was worthwhile."

The band had spent 1990 working on their next album—but without Steve.

"He just wasn't in a fit state to contribute," said Elliott. "We wanted him to get well, so we let him go home to sort himself out. But he just carried on drinking and died."

Let's get rocked

Once again the band had to recover from tragedy. They announced they would carry on and in March 1991 Phil Collen played Steve's guitar parts on their new album to recreate their trademark twin-guitar sound. Explained Phil: "We had made demos of the songs in Holland a couple of years ago and I learnt Steve's guitar parts from there. It was sad and weird listening to him play. It was almost as if his ghost was teaching me the songs. I spent a lot of time in the studio, probably longer than the rest of the band,

Joe Elliot

charts, with a moving tribute to Steve printed on the CD inlay. The music itself was as Leppard as ever—one of its catchiest cuts, 'Let's Get Rocked', was a UK Number 2 hit single in the summer of 1992. The album had taken three years, and although many couldn't understand why it took them so long to make a record, Joe Elliott felt it made all the work worthwhile.

"That's the beauty of spending so much time making a record. You can come back to something four months later and say 'that's horrible'. But with most people it's already in the shops by then. The danger is that your last song will have been through the least evolution, but luckily, with our song 'Let's Get Rocked' it was right there. We recorded the album twice—and everything we recorded the second time was changed three or four times more. It evolved in

perfecting the guitars. They were done three times until it sounded like Def Leppard."

In March 1992 the new album, called *Adrenalize* was released and went straight to the top of the

little bits."

"We never rush anything out," agreed Rick Savage. "We have to be 100 percent happy with the way a record sounds. When an album is so successful, like the last one, the tour has to go on for 15 months as more dates are added. All of a sudden you think, 'I'm 31—where has my life gone?' That's happened a few times to me on this record, but then I think, 'Well what else do you want to do?' "

The band had to produce the album without Mutt Lange who was busy working with Bryan Adams, although Lange helped co-write many of the songs and was credited as executive producer. Most of the production work was done by Mike Shipley who had

Vivian Campbell, of Whitesnake and Dio, was Steve Clark's replacement.

> ## "We had a lot of problems with Steve Clark during 1990. He wasn't in a fit state to contribute to Adrenalize. We told him to go home and get well, but he carried on drinking and died."
>
> *Joe Elliott*

mixed *High'n'Dry* and *Hysteria*, and engineered *Pyromania*.

Vivian steps in

Although Phil Collen had taken over his old pal Steve Clark's guitar parts on the album, he couldn't be expected to re-create the sound of two guitarists live on stage. The band began the search for a replacement. In April 1992 it was announced that Vivian Campbell, a Belfast-born guitarist, would be joining as a full-time member. Campbell had previously worked with American band Dio, and with David Coverdale's Whitesnake. He later joined the Los Angeles-based band Riverdogs and most recently had been with Lou Gramm's Shadow King.

"When we set out on the near impossible task of replacing Steve Clark," said Joe Elliott, "our requirements were simple. We wanted someone with a British passport, a good guitar, a decent voice, and a great personality. In Vivian Campbell we exceeded our wildest expectations. We found a great player, an excellent singer, a terrific human being and a British and Irish passport holder!"

Campbell was delighted to join a

band who had sold some 25 million albums world-wide.

"I consider it a great privilege to be part of a band who, as a fan, I have watched grow from young hopefuls to a bona fide rock institution," gushed the new recruit. "The music's a gas and that level of commitment has been felt already.

"I remember in 1979 when I was a teenager living back in Belfast, when we heard about this band called Def Leppard from Sheffield. There was a real spirit about them on and off stage. After seeing them

> "When we set out to replace Steve Clark, Vivian Campbell exceeded our wildest expectations."
> *Joe Elliott*

play, I remember thinking—I'd really love to be in a band like that!"

Vivian made his debut at the historic Freddie Mercury Tribute Concert held at Wembley Stadium on Easter Monday, April 20, 1992. The band came out to a warm welcome in the afternoon sunshine on a bill that included the ex-members of Queen, Annie Lennox, Guns N' Roses, Ian Hunter, David Bowie and Extreme. Even though the band didn't give one of their best performances, as far as the fans were concerned it was good to see them back.

They played some new material from *Adrenalize* that hadn't been heard by the fans before but, "We were crap," as Phil Collen succinctly put it. "We hadn't done a gig in three years. If we wanted to present the band we definitely did it wrong. We shouldn't have done it there. But we did it because Brian May

113

had asked us and because we're huge Queen fans. At the end of the day I think it did us more harm than good. I think it turned a few people off. For whatever reasons we should have been better. But it wasn't done with that in mind."

Grungy Leppard

Def Leppard then set off on a huge world tour. They played Europe supported by snotty punk metallers Ugly Kid Joe and went to Japan, America and Mexico. The British dates included two homecoming shows at Sheffield's Don Valley Stadium on June 23 and 24, and after that, two nights at London's Earls Court Arena.

But by the mid-Nineties rock music had undergone another of its periodic upheavals. With the arrival

Vivian Campbell enjoys life as a Leppard.

of bands like Nirvana, Pearl Jam and the whole grunge movement Def Leppard were not only regarded as the commercial face of pop metal, they were unfashionable to boot! The band had heard this all before, and took it in their stride. After all, they could still sell out concerts in huge stadiums. At Mexico City they played to a crowd of 20,000 as they finished their *Adrenalize* world tour with their 241st show in 17 months.

Phil Collen told reporter Jerry Ewing: "It's funny to see the backlash for the type of rock music that we play. But having said that, we've been playing sold-out shows and they've been great. So I guess we've been hanging in there. But touring in America is not like it used to be. A bit of the old rock myth has been shattered."

In October 1993 they released a new album, *Retroactive*, which included both new and old material, and on January 4, 1994, 'Action', an old Sweet song dating from 1974. The glam-rock pop song was given a powerful, enthusiastic treatment and Def Leppard enjoyed their first ever chart hit with a cover.

The album included re-mixed and revamped B-sides of past singles like 'Ring Of Fire' and 'Ride Into The Sun', with an acoustic version of 'Miss You In A Heartbeat' and two new recordings—'Desert Song' and 'Fractured Love'.

Many critics felt the album marked a return to the kind of heavier, less self-conscious rock music they played in the days of *High'n'Dry*.

"It's great, like a breath of fresh air," said Phil Collen. "You can get so uptight recording in a certain way. We are a rock band and that's why we started in the first place. This sounds different to anything we have done on the last three albums, since I joined the band in fact. It's great to go back to your roots."

In 1994 Def Leppard promised that their next album would see an end to the old Leppard sound that had been adopted by the likes of Bryan Adams, Bon Jovi and Winger. Phil Collen explained: "Everyone burnt our sound out. I'm not saying we should change because everyone copied us, but we've got quite sick of it too. So it was refreshing to go back to this old stuff we recorded . really innocently."

After more than a decade of achievement and high drama, Def Leppard felt that there was still a strong future for the band, and they were just entering the second phase of their career.

"The general feeling in the band is we want to get back to a more earthy sound," said Rick Savage. "It's still gonna sound like Def Leppard, but back to our roots. *Retroactive* is the direction we're going in."

Def Leppard have been through some extraordinary changes since those far-off days in the Sheffield spoon factory. They may never have been musical giants, but they are true rock'n'rollers.

"We just wanted to put a smile on people's faces. That's all we ever wanted to do," said Joe Elliott—and several million Leppard fans wouldn't argue with that.

Joe and Phil with hero Brian May at the 1992 Freddie Mercury tribute concert.

CHRONOLOGY

- December 8, 1957 Guitarist Phil Collen born in London, UK
- August 1, 1959 Singer Joe Elliott born Sheffield in Yorkshire, UK
- February 16, 1960 Guitarist Pete Willis born in Sheffield, Yorkshire, UK
- April 23, 1960 Guitarist Steve Clark born in Hillsborough, Yorkshire, UK
- December 2, 1960 Bass player Rick Savage born in Sheffield, Yorkshire, UK
- November 1, 1963 Drummer Rick Allen born in Derbyshire, UK
- September, 1977 Deaf Leopard formed by Pete Willis, Rick Savage and Joe Elliott. Name changed to Def Leppard
- January 29, 1978 Guitarist Steve Clark joins Def Leppard during rehearsals in a spoon factory
- July 18, 1978 Band play first show at Westfield School, Sheffield to 150 fans
- September 11, 1978 Def Leppard play the Limit Club, Sheffield, supported by the Human League
- November 25, 1978 Band record three-track EP Getcha Rocks Off, and release it on own Bludgeon Riffola label
- November 27, 1978 Drummer Rick Allen joins the band, replacing Tony Kenning
- January 1979 *Getcha Rocks Off* EP released and played on Radio Hallam
- July 27, 1979 Band play the Rock Garden, Middlesborough and are seen by Phonogram's A&R man Dave Bates
- August 4, 1979 Def Leppard sign to Phonogram's Vertigo label
- September 16, 1979 Def Leppard support Sammy Hagar at Odeon Hammersmith, London
- November 17, 1979 Band's debut single 'Wasted' peaks in UK single chart at Number 61
- March 14, 1980 Debut album *On Through The Night* released
- April 1980 Band signs to American manager Peter Mensch
- May 1980 Def Leppard's first US tour, supporting Pat Travers
- August 24, 1980 Band go down badly at Reading Festival, England
- July 1981 *High'n'Dry* album, produced by Mutt Lange, is released
- July 11, 1982 Guitarist Pete Willis is fired and replaced by Phil Collen of Girl
- January 1983 Third album *Pyromania* released
- February 9, 1983 Phil Collen plays first show with Leppard at London's Marquee Club
- March 18, 1983 Phil Collen makes US debut with Leppard in Atlanta, Georgia
- February 7, 1984 Def Leppard's world tour ends in Bangkok, Thailand
- December 31, 1984 Rick Allen loses left arm in a car crash
- April 1985 Rick Allen rejoins Def Leppard playing specially adapted electronic drum kit
- August 17, 1986 Rick Allen makes first appearance with Def Leppard since accident, at Monsters Of Rock Festival, Castle Donington, England
- August 29, 1987 New Leppard album *Hysteria*

enters UK chart at Number 1
- July 1988 'Pour Some Sugar On Me' single makes Number 2 in US Top 100
- January 21, 1989 'Armageddon It' reaches Number 3 in US Top 100
- February 13, 1989 Group performs live during annual BRIT awards at London's Royal Albert Hall
- September 6, 1989 Group performs live during MTV Video Awards in Los Angeles
- January 8, 1991 Steve Clark found dead at his flat in Chelsea, London, after a night's drinking. He is just 30 years-old
- March 1992 *Adrenalize* album released. Single

'Let's Get Rocked' later Number 2 in UK singles chart
- April 1992 Guitarist Vivian Campbell, ex-Whitesnake, joins Def Leppard to replace the late Steve Clark
- April 20, 1992 Vivian Campbell's debut appearance with the band, playing for Freddie Mercury Tribute Concert at Wembley Stadium
- June 21, 1992 Def Leppard start new world tour in Glasgow, Scotland
- October, 1993 New album *Retroactive* is released
- January 4, 1994 Single 'Action', a cover of the Seventies' hit by Sweet is released

DISCOGRAPHY

Title	Label and CD number	Release date	
Albums			
On Through The Night	UK: Vertigo 8225 332	March 1980	US: Polygram 822533-2
High'n'Dry	UK: Vertigo 818 836 2	July 1981	US: Polygram 12356-2
Pyromania	UK: Mercury 810 308-2	January 1983	US: Polygram 810308-2
Hysteria	UK: Bludgeon Riffola 830 675-2	August 1987	US: Polygram 830675-2
Adrenalize	UK: Bludgeon Riffola 5109782	March 1992	US: Polygram 512185-2
Retroactive	UK: Polygram 5183052	October 1993	US: Polygram 5183052
Singles			
Hysteria	Bludgeon Riffola LEPCD 3		
Armageddon It	Vertigo LEPCD 4		
Love Bites	Bludgeon Riffola LEPCD 5		
Rocket	Bludgeon Riffola LEPCD 6		
Let's Get Rocked	Bludgeon Riffola DEFCD 7		
Tonight	Bludgeon Riffola LEPCD10		
Make Love Like A Man	Bludgeon Riffola LEPCB 7		

INDEX

Picture Acknowledgments
Photographs reproduced by kind
permission of **London Features
International**; **Pictorial Press**/SF
Kaplan,/J Mayer,/Brian Rasic;
Redferns/Fin Costello,/Mick
Hutson,/Neil Kitson,/Ebet
Roberts,/Michael Uhll; **Retna**/M
Diletti,/Adrian Green; **Rex
Features**/Adebari,/Peter
Brooker,/Dave Hogan,/B
Kohmstadt,/Richard Young.
Front cover picture: London Features
International